How to Bake No-Knead Bread in a

Skillet, CorningWare,

Dutch Oven, Covered Baker & More

Updated to Include "Hands-Free" Technique

From the kitchen of
Artisan Bread with Steve

Updated 11.24.2016

By
Steve Gamelin

Now that I have met the standard legal requirements I would like to give my personal exceptions. I understand this is a cookbook and anyone who purchases this book can, (a) print and share the recipes with their friends, as you do with your other cookbooks (of course, it is my hope they too will start to make no-knead bread and buy my cookbooks) and (b) you may share a recipe or two on your website, etc. as long as you note the source and provide instructions on how your audience can acquire this book.
Thanks – Steve

Table of Contents

Letter from Steve 1

Introduction 3

Ingredients 4

    Flour 4

    Salt 5

    Yeast 5

    Water 6

    Flavor Ingredients 6

Technique & Tips 7

    Prep 7

    Combining Ingredients 7

    1st Proofing (bulk fermentation) 7

    Degas, Pull & Stretch 7

    Roll-to-Coat 8

    Garnish & Baste 8

    Divide & Shape 8

    2nd Proofing 8

    Score 9

    Bake 9

    Storing Bread & Dough 9

    Equipment & Bakeware 10

Skillet & More 13

    Skillet 14

Pie Plate 16

Cake Pan 17

Baking Stone 18

Cookie Sheet 19

CorningWare...20

Oblong Loaf (2-1/2 qt Oblong Casserole Dish) 21

Rectangular Loaf (2-1/2 qt Oblong Baker) 23

Boule (2-1/2 qt Round Entrée Baker) 24

Dutch Oven 25

Standard Boule (Dutch Oven) 26

Plump Boule (2.6 qt Ceramic Dutch Oven) 28

Plump Boule (3 qt Cast Iron Dutch Oven) 29

Oval Loaf (3 qt Cast Iron Casserole) 30

Eggplant Shaped Loaf (2.25 qt Cast Iron Casserole Dish) 31

Large Boule (4 qt Cast Iron Braiser) 32

Covered Baker 35

Long Loaf (Long Covered Baker) 36

Boule (Bread Dome) 38

Letter from Steve

The no-knead bread method has revolutionized bread baking. The average family can now have fresh-from-the-oven bakery quality artisan bread in the convenience of their own home with little or no-kneading... Mother Nature does the kneading for you. No-yeast proofing... instant yeast does not need to be proofed in warm water prior to using. No mixer... ingredients can be combined with a spoon. It's almost as easy as making a bowl of *Campbell's* soup.

This is "New Age Bread Baking". I understand what Italian bread, French bread, and baguettes are, and I understand the proper techniques for making those breads, but we live in a new age and we should embrace new ideas. Instead of trying to emulate the bread methods of the past we should focus on our goal... to make great tasting, bakery quality, artisan bread with the methods and techniques that fit our busy schedules.

My Philosophy

I believe in "Smart & Easy". Note, I didn't say fast and cheap. I make no-knead bread because it's the smartest, easiest, way to make bakery quality artisan bread. And I believe my readers and subscribers are attracted to the no-knead method for the same reasons. In response to my readers and subscribers, I strive for convenience and address each recipe from a very practical standpoint... as, I believe, they would want me to develop my recipes.

Smart: In the design of each recipe I try to be smart. I do my best to pick ingredients that are practical, reasonably priced, and easily available. I stay

1

away from complex overlapping flavors and I use ingredients in moderation. More is not always better.

Easy: I look at each step in my recipes and try to simplify it. One of my most successful innovations was using an 8" skillet as a proofing basket. It shapes the dough during proofing and the handle makes it so easy to transport the dough to the baking vessel that even your kids could do it safely.

And I don't have a baker, food stylist or professional photographer... I baked the breads and took the pictures. My pictures are not as good as a professional photographer, but they accurately portray the results you can expect.

My Specialty

My specialty is to take the world's simplest list of ingredients (flour, salt, yeast and water) using the world's easiest bread making method (no mixer, no kneading, no yeast proofing) to create artisan breads that you would be proud to serve your family, friends and guests. One recipe, one method... with minor modifications I can make anything from a boule to an old-fashioned cinnamon roll.

I think you'll enjoy this cookbook.

Steve

"I know when food is supposed to be served in a bowl with a name on it."
Fran Fine - "The Nanny"

Introduction

No Dutch oven... no problem... you can use a skillet, pie plate, cookie sheet, *CorningWare* casserole dish, or a variety of other common household items. You don't need to invest in expensive bakeware to make no-knead bread, but there are subtle differences when baking no-knead bread in a variety of common household items that effects proofing, baking time & temperature and preparation of the bakeware (preheating, etc.).

This cookbook explores the options. It applies the new "hands-free" technique to the world's easiest bread recipe (4 ingredients... no mixer... no kneading... no yeast proofing) and adapts it to various types of bakeware. One recipe... lots of options... It will expand the world of no-knead bread making, stimulate your imagination, and please your palate.

So, let's explore the options, but before we start I want to discuss "Ingredients" and "Tips & Techniques"... if you haven't made no-knead bread before... it's the place to start.

Ingredients

It only takes four ingredients to make bread... flour, salt, yeast and water.

Flour

Flour is the base ingredient of bread and there are four basic types of flour...

(1) <u>Bread flour</u> is designed for yeast bread. It has a higher percentage of gluten which gives artisan bread its airy crumb.

(2) <u>All-purpose flour</u> has less gluten than bread flour. I use all-purpose flour for biscuits, flatbreads, etc. In other words... I use it when I don't want an airy crumb.

(3) <u>Self-rising flour</u> is all-purpose flour with baking soda and baking powder added as leavening agents. It's intended for quick breads... premixed and ready to go. Do not use self-rising flour to make yeast bread. To see the difference between yeast and quick breads you may want to watch <u>Introduction to No-Knead Beer Bread (a.k.a. Artisan Yeast Beer Bread)</u> and <u>Introduction to Quick Beer Bread (a.k.a. Beer Bread Dinner Rolls)</u>.

(4) And there are a variety of <u>specialty flours</u>... whole wheat, rye, and a host of others. Each has its unique flavor and characteristics. In some cases, you can substitute specialty flour for bread flour, but you may need to tweak the recipe because most specialty flours have less gluten. I frequently blend specialty flour with bread flour.

Flour is the primary ingredient... if you don't use the correct flour you won't get the desired results.

Note: To know how many cups of flour there are in a specific bag... it's typically on the side in "Nutritional Facts". For example, this bag reads, "Serving Size 1/4 cup... Serving Per Container about 75". In other words... 18.75 (75 times 1/4). That's the technical answer, but in the real world (measuring cup versus weight) a bag of flour will measure differently based on density (sifted versus unsifted), type of flour (wheat is more dense than bread flour), humidity (flour weighs more on humid days), and all the other variables life and nature have to offer. Thus, there is no single correct answer, but for practical purposes... figure a 5 lb bag of bread flour is 17 to 18 cups.

Salt

While it is possible to make bread without salt... you would be disappointed. There are three basics types of salt...

(1) Most baking recipes are designed to use everyday table salt unless specified otherwise. Unless you're experienced, it is probably smartest to use table salt for your baking needs.

(2) Kosher salt is excellent. I use it when I cook, but a tablespoon of kosher salt does not equal a tablespoon of table salt because kosher salt crystals are larger.

(3) And, I use specialty salt as a garnish... for appearance and taste. For example, I use sea salt to garnish pretzels.

Generally speaking, when salt is added as an ingredient and baked it is difficult to taste the difference between table, kosher and sea salt. When salt is added as a garnish and comes in contact with the taste buds... kosher or specialty salt is an excellent choice.

Yeast

Yeast is the "magic" ingredient which transforms flour and water into dough. My traditional no-knead recipes use 1/4 tsp yeast... I want the dough to rise slowly which allows the dough to develop flavor. My "Turbo" recipes use 1-1/4 tsp yeast... I want a faster rises like traditional bread recipes. There are three basic types of yeast...

(1) The most common is active dry yeast which needs to be proof in warm water prior to being added to flour.

(2) I use instant dry yeast (a.k.a. "instant yeast", "bread machine yeast", "quick rise", "rapid rise", "fast rising", etc.) which does not need to be proofed in warm water. It is a more recent development which is more

potent and reliable... and why worry about proofing yeast if you don't have too.

(3) Some older recipes call for <u>cake yeast</u> (a.k.a. "compressed yeast" or "fresh yeast"), but it's perishable. Most bakers substitute active and instant dry yeast for cake yeast when using older recipes.

The names on the bottles can be confusing. When in doubt, read the instructions and look for one that does not require soaking the yeast in warm water prior to use.

Water
Water hydrates the ingredients and activates the yeast. The no-knead method uses a little more water than the typical recipe... and that's a good thing. It makes it easier to combine the wet and dry ingredients, and contributes to its airy crumb.

(1) I use <u>tap water</u>. It's convenient and easy, but sometimes city water has too much chlorine (chlorine kills yeast).

(2) If your dough does not rise during first proofing you may want to use <u>bottled drinking water</u>.

(3) But, do not use <u>distilled water</u> because the minerals have been removed.

Water is a flavor ingredient, if your water doesn't taste good... use bottled drinking water.

Flavor Ingredients
It only takes four ingredients to make bread... flour, salt, yeast and water, to which a variety of flavor ingredients can be added to make specialty breads such as... honey whole wheat, multi-grain white, rosemary, Mediterranean olive, cinnamon raisin, honey oatmeal, and a host of others.

Technique & Tips

The technique discussed in this section is demonstrated on YouTube in "Easy No-Knead Bread Baked in a Skillet (No Dutch Oven... No Problem)" (released prior to developing "hands-free" technique) and "No-Knead Bread 101 (Includes demonstration of Sesame Seed Bread... Italian, Muffuletta, & Sandwich)."

Prep
Because the traditional method proof for 8 to 24 hours it uses cool water to slow the proofing process, thus the temperature of the bowl is not important.

Combining Ingredients
Pour water in a 3 to 4 qt glass mixing bowl (use warm water and a warm bowl for "Turbo" and cool for traditional). Add salt, yeast, flavor ingredients, etc... and stir to combine (it will insure the ingredients are evenly distributed). Add flour (flour will resist the water and float). Start by stirring the ingredients with the handle end of a plastic spoon drawing the flour from the sides into the middle of bowl (vigorously mixing will not hydrate the flour faster... but it will raise a lot of dust). Within 30 seconds the flour will hydrate and form a shaggy ball. Then scrape dry flour from side of bowl and tumble dough to combine moist flour with dry flour (about 15 seconds). It takes about one minute to combine wet and dry ingredients.

Cover bowl with plastic wrap, place on counter, and proof for 8 to 24 hours.

1st Proofing (bulk fermentation)
The process is called "proofing" because it "proves" the yeast is active.

Bread making is nature at work (yeast is a living organism) and subject to nature. Seasons (summer vs. winter) and weather (heat & humidity) have a direct impact on proofing. In other words, don't worry if your dough varies in size... that's Mother Nature. Just focus on your goal... if the gluten forms (dough develops a stringy nature) and doubles in size... you're good to go.

If your dough does not rise the usual culprits are... outdated yeast or chlorinated water (chlorine kills yeast). Solution, get fresh yeast and/or use bottled drinking water.

If your dough is slow (takes "forever") to rise... your proofing temperature is probably too cool.

Degas, Pull & Stretch
The purpose of degassing, pulling and stretching is to, (a) expel the gases that formed during bulk fermentation, (b) strengthen the dough by realigning and stretching the gluten strands, and (c) stimulate yeast activity for 2nd proofing.

Because no-knead dough is sticky and difficult to handle... I degas, pull & stretch dough by stirring it in the bowl with the handle end of a plastic spoon (like a dough hook). It will reduce the size of the dough ball by 50% making it easier to handle and the process replaces folding and shaping in most cases.

Roll-to-Coat

Before removing the dough from bowl... dust the dough and side of the bowl with flour, then roll-to-coat. The flour will bond to the sticky dough making it easier to handle, but do not roll-to-coat with flour if you're going to garnish or baste.

Garnish & Baste

The purpose of garnishing and basting is to enhance the appearance of the crust, but it isn't necessary. If you decide to garnish and baste there are two techniques... roll-to-coat and skillet method.

Roll-to-Coat Method: Before removing dough from bowl... add ingredients to bowl (on the dough and side of the bowl), then roll to coat. For example, when I garnish honey oatmeal bread... I sprinkle oat in the bowl and on the dough, then roll the dough ball in the oats and they will bond to the sticky dough. This can also be done with seeds, grains, olive oil, egg wash, etc.

Skillet Method: When I want to garnish and/or baste the top of the loaf... I coat the proofing skillet with baste (egg wash, olive oil, vegetable oil, etc.) and sprinkle with the garnish (oats, seeds, grains, etc.). The ingredients will bond with the dough as the dough proofs.

Supporting video: <u>How to Garnish & Baste No-Knead Bread using "Hands-Free" Technique</u>

Divide & Shape

If you're not going to divide the dough... it can go straight from the mixing bowl to the proofing skillet or baking vessel. If you are going to divide and shape the dough... dust the dough and side of the bowl with flour and roll-to-coat, dust work surface with flour, roll the dough ball out of the bowl (excess flour and all) onto the work surface, and divide and shape. I use a plastic bowl scraper to assist in dividing, shaping and carry the dough to the baking vessel. Together they (flour & bowl scraper) make it easier to handle the dough.

2nd Proofing

Originally I proofed for 1 to 2 hours, but over time I have been baking more in bread pans and found shorter proofing times gave better results. I now proof for 30 to 60 minutes.

Tip: To fit bread making into your schedule... you can extend 2nd proofing times, but you don't want the dough to exceed the size of the baking vessel. If you're using a large baking vessel (Dutch oven, etc.) it's never a problem, but if you're using a bread pan don't allow the dough to exceed the sides of the pan before baking or your loaf will droop over the sides and be less attractive. But, always bake it... it will still be delicious.

Score

The purpose of scoring dough is to provide seams to control where the crust will split during "oven spring", but it isn't necessary to score dough. If you do decide to score your loaf you may want to use a scissors (no-knead dough is very moist and more likely to stretch than slice). Personally, I place the dough in the baking vessel seam side up... the dough will split at the seam during "oven spring" which gives the loaf a nice rustic appearance.

Bake

Baking Time: Bread is done when it reaches an internal temperature of 185 to 220 degrees F. and the crumb (inside of the bread) isn't doughy. Baking times in my recipes are designed to give bread an internal temperature of 200 to 205 degrees F, but ovens vary and you may need to adjust your baking times slightly.

No-Stick Spray: Most bakeware has a non-stick surface, but it is safest to spray your bakeware unless you are fully confident your bread won't stick.

Ovens: Ovens aren't always accurate. I check the temperature of ovens and bakeware. Ovens with a digital readout that displays the temperature as they preheat are typically very accurate, but ovens that say they will be at temperature in a specific number of minutes are not always accurate. My point is... you will get the best results if you learn the character and nature of your oven.

Oven Rack: Generally speaking you want to bake bread and rolls in the middle or lower third of the oven, but it isn't critical. Just keep them away from the upper heating element or they may brown a little too quickly.

Oven Spring: When dough is first put into the oven it will increase in size by as much as a third in a matter of minutes because, (a) gases trapped in the dough will expand, (b) moisture will turn into steam and try to push its way out, and (c) yeast will become highly active converting sugars into gases. The steam and gases work together to create "oven spring". Once the internal temperature of the bread reaches 120 degrees F... the yeast will begin to die and the crust will harden.

Storing Bread & Dough

After allowing bread to cool... it can be wrapped in plastic wrap, or stored in a zip-lock plastic bag, or plastic bread bags (available on the web). If you wish to keep bread for a longer period of time... slice it into portions and freeze them in a zip-lock freezer bag (remove excess air). Do not store bread in the refrigerator. Bread goes stale faster in the refrigerator.

If you wish to save dough... divide it into portions, drizzle each portion with olive oil, place in zip-lock bag, remove excess air, and refrigerate for up to two days or freeze for up to two months. To thaw dough... move dough from freezer to refrigerator the day before (12 or more hours), then place on counter for 30 minutes before use to come to room temperature.

Equipment & Bakeware

Bowl for Mixing: You can use any 3 to 4 qt bowl. I use a 3-1/2 qt glass bowl because, (a) there's ample room for the dough to expand, (b) plastic wrap sticks to glass, and (c) I don't want the rim of my bowl to exceed the width of the plastic wrap.

Measuring Spoons: I'm sure you already have measuring spoons in the kitchen... they will work just fine. If you're going to buy new, I prefer oval versus round because an oval shape will fit into jars and containers more easily.

Measuring Cups: Dry measuring cups are designed to be filled to the top and leveled. Liquid measuring cups have a pour spout and are designed to be filled to the gradations on the side (neither measures weight). Because of their design and a slight difference in volume, it is best to use the appropriate measuring cup.

Note: U.S. and metric measuring cups may be used interchangeably... there is only a slight difference (±3%). More importantly, the ingredients of a recipe measured with a set (U.S. or metric) will have their volumes in the same proportion to one another.

Spoon for Combining Wet and Dry Ingredients: A spoon is an excellent tool for combining wet and dry ingredients. Surprisingly, I found the handle end of a plastic spoon worked best for me because, I didn't have a big clump on the end like some of my other mixing utensils (which makes it easier to stir and manipulate the dough). And when you think about it... mixers don't use a paddle to mix dough, they use a hook which looks a lot like the handle end of my spoon.

Silicon Baking Mat: Silicone baking mats are very useful... I use them as reusable parchment paper (they're environmentally friendly). Silicone baking mats serve two purposes... (a) as a work surface for folding and shaping (they have excellent non-stick properties), and (b) as a baking mat... specifically when the dough is difficult to move after folding and shaping. And I slide a cookie sheet under the mat before baking (it makes it easier to put the mat into and take it out of the oven).

Spatula: I use a spatula to scrape the sides of the bowl to get the last bits of flour incorporated into the dough.

Plastic Bowl Scraper: I use a plastic bowl scraper verses a metal dough scraper because it's the better multi-tasker. I use the bowl scraper to (a) fold, shape, and divide the dough, (b) assist in transporting the dough to the proofing vessel, (c) scrape excess flour off the work surface, (d) scrape excess flour out of the bowl (after all it is a bowl scraper), and (e) scrape any remaining bits in the sink towards the disposal. It's a useful multi-tasker and you can't do all those tasks with a metal cough scraper.

Timer: I'm sure you already have a timer and it will work just fine. If you're thinking about a new one... I prefer digital because they're more accurate.

Proofing Baskets & Vessels: The purpose of a proofing basket or vessel is to pre-shape the dough prior to baking (dough will spread if it isn't contained). Because no-knead dough has a tendency to stick to the lining of proofing baskets... I use common household items as proofing vessels. For example, I use an 8" skillet (with no-stick spray) to pre-shape dough when baking in a Dutch oven. It shapes the dough during proofing, and the handle makes it easy to carry the dough and put it in the hot Dutch oven safely.

You can also proof dough in the baking vessel if it doesn't have to be preheated. For example, standard loaves are typically proof and baked in the bread pan where your bread pan shapes the loaf during proofing and baking. You can use this same principle for shaping and baking rolls and buns.

Baking Vessels: Baking vessels come in a variety of sizes, shapes and materials. You can change the appearance of the loaf by sampling changing the baking vessel.

Plastic Wrap & Proofing Towel: I use plastic wrap for 1st proofing and a lint-free towel for 2nd proofing. Plastic wrap protects dough for longer proofing times and can be used to create a favorable proofing environment (solar effect).

Cooling Rack: The purpose of a cooling rack is to expose the bottom of the loaf during the cooling process.

Bread Bags: I use plastic bread bags to store bread after they have cooled. And they're great for packaging bread as gifts. I also use paper bags as gifts when the loaf is still warm and I don't want to trap the moisture in a plastic bag... it gives a nice natural appearance.

10" Flat Whisk: I use a flat whisk to combine dry ingredients with yogurt... a flat whisk will slice through yogurt forming small clump. If you use a balloon whisk a big lump will form inside the balloon.

Pastry/Pizza Roller: When you watch shows they hand shape and toss pizza dough, but I find it more practical to use a pastry/pizza roller. It is also useful when shaping flatbread and cinnamon rolls.

Bakers have known for years that
bread benefits from long proofing times.
The no-knead method takes advantage of this principle.
It uses a minimum amount of yeast
and long proofing time to develop flavor.
Meanwhile, the long proofing time
replaces the arduous task of kneading...
Mother Nature does the work for you.

It's smart... it's easy... it's delicious.

Skillet & More

You don't have to invest in bakeware to make no-knead bread. To make my point, I used the "traditional" no-knead bread recipe and "hands-free" technique to bake no-knead bread in a skillet, pie plate, and cake pan… and on a baking stone and cookie sheet to demonstrate you can use common everyday bakeware that you already have to bake no-knead bread.

I will use 1 recipe and 5 different baking vessels/methods.

The nature of uncovered bakeware…
I reduced the oven temperature from 450 to 400 degrees F and increased the baking time from 30 to 40 minutes from the "traditional" no-knead recipe because the dynamics of baking in an uncovered baker (open oven) is different from the Dutch oven. The Dutch oven creates a "screaming" hot environment inside the baking vessel while an on covered baker (skillet, etc.) uses the oven box to trap the moisture. The lower temperature and longer baking time allows more time for "oven bounce" and the crumb will reach 200 degrees F at the same time that the crust is medium brown.

Pros…
You don't need to invest in expensive bakeware.

Cons…
None

Skillet
I use an 8" *Lodge* cast iron skillet to shape this loaf, but you can use any 8" to 10-1/2" oven safe skillet (make sure the handle is oven safe).

Recipe changes...
I want to include garnishing in the recipe because it is so easy when you're using the "roll-to-coat" method, but it is optional.
I didn't score the loaf... I let Mother Nature decide.

Pros...
You don't need to invest in expensive bakeware.
You can create different sizes and shapes. A smaller 8" skillet will constrain the dough during oven bounce and force the dough to expand upwards and give you a tall plump boule, while a larger 10-1/2" skillet will allow the dough to expand outwards filling the skillet and give you a broad low profile boule.

Cons...
None

Uncovered Bakeware (all types & shapes)

Pour water into a 3 to 4 qt glass mixing bowl.

> 12 oz cool Water

Add salt and yeast... give a quick stir to combine.

> 1-1/2 tsp Salt
> 1/4 tsp Instant Yeast

Add flour... stir until dough forms a shaggy ball, scrape dry flour from side of bowl, then tumble dough to combine moist flour with dry flour.

> 3 cups Bread Flour

Cover bowl with plastic wrap, place in a warm draft-free location, and proof for 8 to 24 hours.

8 to 24 hours later

When dough has risen and developed its gluten structure... spray baking vessel with no-stick cooking spray and set aside.

"Degas, pull and stretch"... stick handle end of a plastic spoon in the dough and stir (dough will form a sticky ball). Then, scrape side of bowl to get remainder of the dough into the sticky dough ball.

Garnish (optional)... sprinkle dough ball and side of bowl with sesame seeds and roll-to-coat.

> 2 Tbsp Sesame Seeds

Roll dough out of bowl into baking vessel.

Place in a warm draft-free location, cover with a lint-free towel, and proof for 30 to 60 minutes.

Before dough is fully proofed...

Move rack to middle of oven and pre-heat to 400 degrees F.

30 to 60 minutes later

When oven has come to temperature... place baking vessel in oven and bake for 40 minutes.

40 minutes later

Gently turn bread out on work surface and place on cooling rack.

Pie Plate

And if you don't have a skillet... you can use a metal or glass pie plate.

Recipe changes...

I didn't garnish the loaf.

Pros...

You don't need to invest in expensive bakeware.

Pie plate will bevel the sides and give you a nice boule.

Cons...

None

Cake Pan

And there's very little difference between a metal bread pan and cake pan... one gives you a loaf and the other gives you a boule.

Recipe changes...

I didn't garnish the loaf.

Pros...

You don't need to invest in expensive bakeware.

Cons...

I prefer the bevel the sides I get from a pie plate.

Baking Stone

Personally... I think it's fun to bake directly on a baking stone... you never know what shape you'll get.

Recipe changes...

Preheat baking stone in oven, proof dough in 8" skillet, and use proofing skillet to place the dough in middle of baking stone.

Bake it for 30 to 35 minutes depending on how you like your crust (the baking time was reduced because the heat from the baking stone).

Pros...

Rustic appearance

Cons...

You need to have a baking stone.

Cookie Sheet
And if you don't have a baking stone... you can bake no-knead bread on a cookie sheet.

Recipe changes...
Proof dough in 8" skillet (you don't have to use a proofing skillet... you can proof directly on the cookie sheet, but the dough will spread and give you a flatter boule) and use proofing skillet to place the dough in middle and bake on cookie sheet.

Pros...
You don't need a baking stone.
Rustic appearance

Cons...
None

CorningWare

CorningWare is an inexpensive substitute for the "Dutch oven"... and you may already have one around the house. Just like the Dutch oven... it is oven save and has excellent heat retention properties.

I will use 1 recipe and 3 different casserole dishes/bakers.

The nature of *CorningWare*...

CorningWare comes in various sizes and shapes, thus by changing the size and shape of your baker you can change the shape of your loaf. I have three 2-1/2 qt bakers. Each gives me a unique shape because the sides control the shape during "oven spring". And the older *CorningWare* dishes with the heaver lids do a better job of trapping the heat.

Pros...

You don't have to invest in expensive bakeware.
Versatility of shape... round, oval, and rectangular.

Cons...

CorningWare is oven safe and has a nonporous surface. It will trap the moisture from the dough and give your loaf an excellent crust, but the glazed finish will give your loaves a soft bottom. Solution... take the loaf out of the baking vessel after baking for 30 minutes with the top on and put it back in the oven on the oven rack (or a cookie sheet, baking stone, etc.) to finish baking for the last 5 to 15 minutes.

Note: Personally, I store my baking stone in the oven (they're large, heavy, hot after use, and difficult to store). The good news is... the baking stone is the perfect bakeware for finishing a loaf that has a soft bottom, but it is not necessary to have the baking stone in the oven... the oven rack (or cookie sheet) will do just fine.

Oblong Loaf (2-1/2 qt Oblong Casserole Dish)

The 2-1/2 qt *CorningWare* French White oblong covered casserole dish (9" x 13" x 2-1/2") will give you a classic oval shape.

Recipe changes...

None

Pros...

You don't need to invest in expensive bakeware.
The shape of the dish will give you a nice oval loaf.

Cons...

Loaf should be removed from the dish and baked on the oven rack for the last 5 to 15 minutes.
On occasion, the loaf will rise during "oven spring" and it may touch the lid, but no one has noticed the slight dimple on the top of the loaf.

CorningWare (all shapes)

Pour water into a 3 to 4 qt glass mixing bowl.

> 12 oz cool Water

Add salt and yeast... give a quick stir to combine.

> 1-1/2 tsp Salt

> 1/4 tsp Instant Yeast

Add flour... stir until dough forms a shaggy ball, scrape dry flour from side of bowl, then tumble dough to combine moist flour with dry flour.

> 3 cups Bread Flour

Cover bowl with plastic wrap, place in a warm draft-free location, and proof for 8 to 24 hours.

8 to 24 hours later (CorningWare)

When dough has risen and developed its gluten structure... spray an 8" proofing skillet with no-stick cooking spray and set aside.

"Degas, pull and stretch"... stick handle end of a plastic spoon in the dough and stir (dough will form a sticky ball). Then, scrape side of bowl to get remainder of the dough into the sticky dough ball.

Roll dough out of bowl into proofing skillet.

Place in a warm draft-free location, cover with a lint-free towel, and proof for 30 to 60 minutes.

Before dough is fully proofed...

Move rack to lower third of oven, place baking vessel in oven, and pre-heat to 450 degrees F.

30 to 60 minutes later

When oven has come to temperature... remove baking vessel from oven, spray with no-stick cooking spray, transfer dough from proofing skillet to baking vessel, shake to center, and bake for 30 minutes with the top on.

30 minutes later

After baking for 30 minutes with the top on... take the *CorningWare* dish out of the oven, remove the loaf and put the loaf back in the oven to bake for an additional 5 to 15 minutes to finish the crust.

5 to 15 minutes later

Remove loaf from oven and place on cooling rack.

Rectangular Loaf (2-1/2 qt Oblong Baker)

The 2-1/2 qt *CorningWare* etch Eggplant oblong baker with lid (7" x 10" x 3") will give you a very nice rectangular loaf... ideal for sandwiches and toast.

Recipe changes...

None

Pros...

You don't need to invest in expensive bakeware.
The shape of the baker will give you a nice rectangular loaf.

Cons...

Loaf should be removed from the dish and baked on the oven rack for the last 5 to 15 minutes.

Boule (2-1/2 qt Round Entrée Baker)

The 2-1/2 qt *CorningWare* French White round entrée baker (7.5" x 3.5") is a nice baking vessel... its heavy lid will retain heat better than the newer thin covers. It will do an excellent job of shaping your loaf, but I gravitate towards the 3 qt *Lodge* or 2.6 qt *Emile Henry* when I want a boule. From a cost standpoint, this is an excellent option.

Recipe changes...

None

Pros...

You don't need to invest in expensive bakeware.
The shape of the baker will give you a nice boule... a lot like a Dutch oven.

Cons...

Loaf should be removed from the dish and baked on the oven rack for the last 5 to 15 minutes.

Dutch Oven

A Dutch oven is a heavy cooking pot (usually cast iron) with a lid. It is frequently used for braising, soups and stews. The reason we call them Dutch ovens is because the Dutch perfected the method of manufacturing them in the late 1600's. In today's world, the Dutch oven is the perfect partner for no-knead bread where the purpose of the Dutch oven is to emulate a baker's oven by trapping the moisture from the dough, thus creating steam in a "screaming" hot, enclosed environment.

I will use 2 recipes and 6 different Dutch ovens.

The nature of Dutch ovens...
Dutch ovens come in various sizes and shapes. Thus by changing the size and shape of your Dutch oven you can change the shape of your loaf.

Pros...
The "traditional" no-knead bread recipe was designed to be baked in a cast iron Dutch oven.

Cons...
None

Standard Boule (Dutch Oven)

This is the standard baking vessel for which the "traditional" no-knead recipe was designed. The 5 qt Dutch oven will give you a low profile boule... a very traditional shape for artisan bread. If you want to emulate the artisan style, bake the loaf with the top off for 15 to 30 minutes to develop a harder more rustic crust. I use our old 5 qt *Circulon* hard-anodized aluminum nonstick Dutch oven (9-1/2") to shape this loaf.

Recipe changes...

None

Pros...

Traditional shape

Cons...

None

Standard Boule (Dutch Oven)

Pour water into a 3 to 4 qt glass mixing bowl.

<u>12 oz cool Water</u>

Add salt and yeast... give a quick stir to combine.

<u>1-1/2 tsp Salt</u>

<u>1/4 tsp Instant Yeast</u>

Add flour... stir until dough forms a shaggy ball, scrape dry flour from side of bowl, then tumble dough to combine moist flour with dry flour.

<u>3 cups Bread Flour</u>

Cover bowl with plastic wrap, place in a warm draft-free location, and proof for 8 to 24 hours.

8 to 24 hours later (Dutch oven)

When dough has risen and developed its gluten structure... spray an 8" proofing skillet with no-stick cooking spray and set aside.

"Degas, pull and stretch"... stick handle end of a plastic spoon in the dough and stir (dough will form a sticky ball). Then, scrape side of bowl to get remainder of the dough into the sticky dough ball.

Roll dough out of bowl into proofing skillet.

Place in a warm draft-free location, cover with a lint-free towel, and proof for 30 to 60 minutes.

Before dough is fully proofed...

Move rack to lower third of oven, place baking vessel in oven, and pre-heat to 450 degrees F.

30 to 60 minutes later

When oven has come to temperature... remove baking vessel from oven, transfer dough from proofing skillet to baking vessel, shake to center, and bake for 30 minutes with the top on and 3 to 15 minutes with the top off depending on how rustic (hard) you like your crust.

33 to 45 minutes later

Gently turn loaf out on work surface and place on cooling rack.

Plump Boule (2.6 qt Ceramic Dutch Oven)
I used a 2.6 qt *Emile Henry* flame top ceramic Dutch oven (8") to shape this loaf.

Recipe changes...
Generally speaking, it isn't necessary to spray cast iron with no-stick cooking spray, but the *Emile Henry* is ceramic and as it has aged the finish has warn and the dough sticks. So I spray it after preheating just before inserting the dough.

Pros...
I like the shape the *Emile Henry* gives my loaves. The sides of the *Emile Henry* are tapered which trims the sides of the loaf... a little smaller base, a little taller, a nicely shaped boule.

Cons...
But the loaf can have a soft bottom... ceramic doesn't bake as hot as cast iron. It's the nature of ceramic which is why I take the loaf out of the *Emile Henry* to bake on the oven rack for the last 3 to 15 minutes.

Note: Personally, I store my baking stone in the oven (they're large, heavy, hot after use, and difficult to store). The good news is... the baking stone is the perfect bakeware for finishing a loaf that has a soft bottom, but it is not necessary to have the baking stone in the oven... the oven rack (or cookie sheet) will do just fine.

Plump Boule (3 qt Cast Iron Dutch Oven)
I used a 3 qt *Cuisinart* enameled cast iron Dutch oven (8") to shape this loaf.

Recipe changes...
None

Pros...
The 3 qt Dutch oven will give you a nice plump boule, 8" round that is 1" to 2" taller than the 5 qt Dutch oven, a nice shape for sandwiches and toast.

Cons...
None, but I prefer the shape the *Emile Henry* gives my loaves.

Oval Loaf (3 qt Cast Iron Casserole)
I used a 3 qt *KitchenAid* traditional cast iron casserole (8-1/2"x10"x3") to shape this loaf.

Recipe changes...
None

Pros...
The oval shape gives the loaf a little different shape and the other cast iron Dutch ovens.
Cast iron does a better job of finishing the bottom of the loaf compared to the *CorningWare* oblong casserole dish.

Cons...
But the loaf has a lower profile than the one baked in the oval *CorningWare* 2-1/2 qt oblong casserole dish because it's 1" wider.

Eggplant Shaped Loaf (2.25 qt Cast Iron Casserole Dish)
Unique and classic... I used a 2.25 qt *Le Creuset* 2.25 qt eggplant shaped enamel cast iron covered casserole (10-1/2 x Irregular x 5") to shape this loaf.

Recipe changes...
None

Pros...
Unique shape

Cons...
The eggplant shape casserole dish is no longer available, but it is an excellent example of using a baking vessel to shape a loaf. The point is... look around your kitchen, you may have a uniquely shaped oven-safe casserole dish that you could use.

Large Boule (4 qt Cast Iron Braiser)

Want a larger boule... the *Giada de Laurentiis* 4 qt braiser has a larger diameter (10-3/4") than the average 5 qt Dutch oven (10").

Recipe changes...

To take full advantage of its size I increased the recipe's ingredients by 50%. The dough will fit in the 3-1/2 qt glass mixing bowl, but you will need to use a 10" non-stick skillet for 2nd proofing and you need to increase baking time by 10 minutes to account for its larger size. I use a 4 qt *Giada de Laurentiis* cast iron braiser pan with lid (10-3/4" x 2-1/2") to shape this loaf.

Pros...

The braiser is identical in use and performance to any other cast iron Dutch oven. If there is any reason you would want to make a larger boule, this is an excellent option.

Cons...

Too large for the "traditional" no-knead recipe.

Large Boule (4 qt Cast Iron Braiser)

Pour water into a 3-1/2 to 4 qt glass mixing bowl.

<u>18 oz cool Water</u>

Add salt and yeast... give a quick stir to combine.

<u>2-1/2 tsp Salt</u>

<u>1/2 tsp Instant Yeast</u>

Add flour... stir until dough forms a shaggy ball, scrape dry flour from side of bowl, then tumble dough to combine moist flour with dry flour.

<u>4-1/2 cups Bread Flour</u>

Cover bowl with plastic wrap, place in a warm draft-free location, and proof for 8 to 24 hours.

8 to 24 hours later (Dutch oven)

When dough has risen and developed its gluten structure... spray a 10" proofing skillet with no-stick cooking spray and set aside.

"Degas, pull and stretch"... stick handle end of a plastic spoon in the dough and stir (dough will form a sticky ball). Then, scrape side of bowl to get remainder of the dough into the sticky dough ball.

Roll dough out of bowl into proofing skillet.

Place in a warm draft-free location, cover with a lint-free towel, and proof for 30 to 60 minutes.

Before dough is fully proofed...

Move rack to lower third of oven, place baking vessel in oven, and pre-heat to 450 degrees F.

30 to 60 minutes later

When oven has come to temperature... remove baking vessel from oven, transfer dough from proofing skillet to baking vessel, shake to center, and bake for 40 minutes with the top on and 3 to 15 minutes with the top off depending on how rustic (hard) you like your crust.

40 to 55 minutes later

Gently turn loaf out on work surface and place on cooling rack.

We are attracted to no-knead bread because
it's easy and convenient,
but dough can be difficult to shape.
This cookbook is about using
bakeware to shape the dough.
Just plop the dough into the bakeware of your choice,
let Mother Nature do her magic,
and the dough will take on the shape of the bakeware.
Poof, you'll have a perfectly shaped loaf.

Covered Baker

Bread bakers are designed to emulate traditional bread making in an adobe oven. There are three basic designs... round bread cloche, bread dome and long covered baker. I have a bread dome and long covered baker. The round bread cloche and bread dome are designed to make a boule and the long covered baker is designed to make long loaves.

I will use 2 recipes... 1 for each covered baker because of the process.

The nature of covered bakers...
Sassafras superstone is sometimes referred to as "natural stone" bakeware. It can be left natural or glazed. When it is left natural it needs to be seasoned.

Pros...
Covered bakers are designed to shape bread. They are among my favorites.

Cons...
Unglazed natural stone needs to be seasoned.

Long Loaf (Long Covered Baker)

I used our *Sassafras* superstone long covered baker (13-1/2" x 4-1/2" x 2-1/2") to shape this loaf.

Pros...

I love the shape our *Sassafras* superstone long covered baker (13-1/2" x 4-1/2" x 2-1/2") gives my loaves. If I want a long loaf... it's #1. Its narrow sides prevent the dough from expanding outward and force it to expand in length and height during "oven spring".

Cons...

Baker needs to be seasoned.

Long Loaf (Long Covered Baker)
Pour water into a 3 to 4 qt glass mixing bowl.

> 12 oz cool Water

Add salt and yeast... give a quick stir to combine.

> 1-1/2 tsp Salt

> 1/4 tsp Instant Yeast

Add flour... stir until dough forms a shaggy ball, scrape dry flour from side of bowl, then tumble dough to combine moist flour with dry flour.

> 3 cups Bread Flour

Cover bowl with plastic wrap, place in a warm draft-free location, and proof for 8 to 24 hours.

8 to 24 hours later (long covered baker)
When dough has risen and developed its gluten structure... spray bottom of baker with no-stick spray and set aside.

"Degas, pull and stretch"... stick handle end of a plastic spoon in the dough and stir (dough will form a sticky ball). Then, scrape side of bowl to get remainder of the dough into the sticky dough ball.

"Roll-to-coat"... sprinkle dough ball and side of bowl with flour and roll-to-coat (dusting dough ball with flour will make it easier to handle and shape the dough for the baker).

> 2 Tbsp Bread Flour

Dust work surface with flour, roll dough (and excess flour) out of bowl onto work surface, roll dough on work surface in flour to shape, and place in baker.

Cover with lid, place in a warm draft-free location, and proof for 30 to 60 minutes.

Before dough is fully proofed...
Move rack to lower third of the oven and pre-heat to 400 degrees F (baker does not have to be preheated).

30 to 60 minutes later
When oven has come to temperature... place baker in oven and bake for 40 minutes with the top on.

40 minutes later
Take baker out of the oven, remove top, and place back in the oven for 3 to 15 minutes to finish the crust... depending on how rustic (hard) you like your crust.

3 to 15 minutes later
Gently turn loaf out on work surface and place on cooling rack.

Boule (Bread Dome)
The Sassafras superstone bread dome (8-1/2" x 4-1/2") was not designed for the traditional no-knead method... it's glazed and has a vent hole which is just fine... it should be used as it was intended.

I adapted the baking method to take advantage of the design. I proof the dough in the baker and put it in after preheating the oven (note... I used a different baking time and temperature for this method). I also garnish the loaf with sesame seeds. It makes the loaf look gorgeous and adds a really nice flavor and texture to the crust.

Pros...
The bread dome was designed to shape a boule and does an excellent job.

Cons...
None

Boule (Bread Dome)

Pour water into a 3 to 4 qt glass mixing bowl.

> 12 oz cool Water

Add salt and yeast... give a quick stir to combine.

> 1-1/2 tsp Salt
> 1/4 tsp Instant Yeast

Add flour... stir until dough forms a shaggy ball, scrape dry flour from side of bowl, then tumble dough to combine moist flour with dry flour.

> 3 cups Bread Flour

Cover bowl with plastic wrap, place in a warm draft-free location, and proof for 8 to 24 hours.

8 to 24 hours later (bread dome | garnish)

When dough has risen and developed its gluten structure... spray bottom of bread dome with no-stick spray and set aside.

"Degas, pull and stretch"... stick handle end of a plastic spoon in the dough and stir (dough will form a sticky ball). Then, scrape side of bowl to get remainder of the dough into the sticky dough ball.

"Garnish" (optional)... sprinkle dough ball and side of bowl with seeds and roll-to-coat.

> 2 Tbsp Sesame Seeds

Roll dough out of bowl into bread dome, cover with lid, place in a warm draft-free location, and proof for 30 to 60 minutes.

Before dough is fully proofed...

Move rack to lower third of the oven and pre-heat to 400 degrees F (bread dome does not have to be preheated).

30 to 60 minutes later

When oven has come to temperature... place bread dome in oven and bake for 40 minutes with the top on.

40 minutes later

Take bread dome out of the oven, remove top, and place back in the oven for 3 to 15 minutes to finish the crust... depending on how rustic (hard) you like your crust.

3 to 15 minutes later

Gently turn loaf out on work surface and place on cooling rack.

Made in the USA
Lexington, KY
01 September 2017